DANIEL TIGER'S NEIGHBORHOOD®

The Official
COOKBOOK

DANIEL TIGER'S NEIGHBORHOOD®

The Official

COOKBOOK

Recipes by Rebecca Woods
Words by Kate Lloyd

Andrews McMeel
PUBLISHING®

Contents

Hi, neighbor! We hope you have fun making these recipes!

They're full of goodness and taste deee-licious!

DIETARY SYMBOLS

Following a vegetarian, vegan, or gluten-free diet? Look out for these symbols through this book, they'll tell you how to easily adapt the recipe to make it suitable for you.

V Suitable for vegetarians

VG Suitable for vegans

GF Suitable for those on a gluten-free diet

DF Suitable for those on a dairy-free diet

Hi, Neighbor!

Welcome to *The Official Daniel Tiger's Neighborhood Cookbook!*

There's so much to do, so much to see in this grr-ific recipe book. Won't you cook along with us?

From Dad Tiger's Strawberry Heart Pancakes and O the Owl's Rice Paper Shrimp Rolls to Miss Elaina's Veggie Spaghetti Dinner and Daniel Tiger's (Peach-Free) Banana Bread Muffins, this official cookbook is packed with healthy, wholesome, and deee-licious ideas for breakfast, lunch, dinner, snacks, and more.

In addition to being yummy in your tummy, these recipes are also designed to get children involved in the kitchen, with simple-to-follow instructions that families will love working through together and lots of friendly contributions from Daniel and his neighbors, too.

Cooking with children has so many benefits, from developing confidence and an appreciation for homemade meals to expanding tastebuds and boosting skills such as numeracy, language, and cultural awareness. Kids will come away with "such a good feeling, a very good feeling," as Daniel Tiger would say—and grown-ups will, too.

To suit all tastes, these recipes have been developed to be flexible. For example, Queen Sara's Lunchbox Kebobs on page 38 are made with strips of thick-cut ham, but we explain in a "tip box" how you can easily make them vegetarian or vegan.

And there's lots of other helpful advice scattered throughout, as well, from suggestions for toppings to what best to serve the dish with—crunchy bread is a must with The Tigers' Family Veggie Campfire Stew, for example (page 60).

At the back of the book, you'll even find space to write down your shared family thoughts on the recipes, from the messiest to the yummiest to the most fun to cook.

So, neighbor, what are you waiting for? It's time to mixa, mixa, mixa!

Kitchen Safety Rules

Count with Daniel Tiger as you learn how to stay safe in the kitchen...

1 Before you start cooking, give your hands a good wash.

2 Clean all kitchen surfaces.

3 Roll up sleeves, tie back long hair, and wear an apron to protect your clothes.

4 Read through your chosen recipe, making sure you have everything you need.

5 If your recipe includes fruit and veggies, make sure you wash them well.

6 Never start to cook without a grown-up present.

7 Always ask an adult before handling knives or going near hot things such as an oven or saucepan.

8 Never run in the kitchen.

It's very important to wash your hands before cooking. Turn the page to find out how to wash them properly.

9 Never taste food when it's piping hot or partway cooked.

10 Tidy up when you have finished.

PREVENTING CHOKING: ADVICE FOR GROWN-UPS
Small, sticky, or hard foods such as grapes, peanut butter, and nuts can cause children to choke. To keep your child safe, make sure all potentially problematic foods are ground down, finely chopped, or cut into very small pieces before serving. Encourage your child to always sit down when eating—even if it's just a snack—and to chew their food thoroughly. Young children should always be supervised by an adult during mealtimes.

How to Wash Your Hands Properly

It's always important to wash your hands before, during, and after cooking.

Unwashed hands have germs on them, which can spread to the food you're preparing, as well as work surfaces and kitchen equipment. You can't see these germs because they're invisible, but they are there and can cause things like bad tummies. Washing your hands properly washes these germs away.

FIVE STEPS TO CLEAN HANDS!

1 Wet your hands with clean, running water—it can be hot or cold, it doesn't matter!

2 Apply soap and rub your hands together firmly, making sure to lather the front and back, as well as between your fingers, under your nails, and even your wrists.

3 Scrub your hands for 20 seconds, counting out loud as you do so.

4 Rinse your hands under clean, running water.

5 Dry your hands with a clean towel or air-dry them (this means waving them around until they're not wet anymore—try it, it's fun!)

NOW YOU'RE READY TO COOK!

Trying New Foods Is Fun!

Let's make believe... that we're vegetable tasters!

When Katerina Kittycat was feeling scared about trying vegetables, Teacher Harriet and Katerina's friends sang her this song:

"We gotta try new food 'cause it might taste good."

It worked! Encouraged by Daniel Tiger, Prince Wednesday, and Miss Elaina, Katerina tried the bell peppers and loved their crispy and sweet taste. "Yum, yum, peppers are my new favorite," she said happily.

In this book, you'll find lots of foods that you perhaps haven't tried before. You might feel nervous about tasting them, because they look, smell, or feel a bit different from what you're used to. But we have an idea! When there's something new on your plate, why not sing Teacher Harriet's song with your grown-up? Then, when you're feeling brave enough, give the new food a go!

Even if you don't like it—Katerina didn't like the carrots, remember?—you can feel proud of yourself for trying. And you never know, you might like it as much as Daniel likes strawberries and Katerina likes bell peppers!

> I tried! Yay for me, meow meow!

> Which foods do you want to try? I hope they taste good!

Did you know there are five main food groups? These are:

- Fruit and vegetables
- Starchy carbohydrates such as potatoes, bread, rice, and pasta
- Proteins such as beans, fish, eggs, and meat
- Dairy and dairy alternatives
- Healthy fats such as oils and spreads

A balanced diet provides your body with the nutrients it needs to work effectively—and will make you feel great.

Allergy Information

Did you know that food allergies are really common? It's estimated that 1 in 13 children in the United States are allergic to one or more foods.

The most common allergens are wheat, milk, egg, soy, peanuts, tree nuts, fish, and shellfish, but almost any food can cause an allergic reaction.

When Daniel Tiger tries peaches for the first time, for example, he thinks they are yummy and juicy, but then his face and legs begin to itch, and his tummy starts to hurt.

Dad Tiger takes Daniel to visit Dr. Anna to find out what's making him feel this way. After examining him and asking him some questions, Dr. Anna tells Daniel that he is allergic to peaches.

Dr. Anna explains that an allergy is when your body doesn't like something.
To keep himself safe, **Daniel must follow three new rules:**

1 Don't eat the food you are allergic to.

2 If you don't feel well, tell a grown-up.

3 Ask before you eat something new.

If you have an allergy, try following these rules as well. They are designed to keep you feeling grr-ific.

It's also worth remembering that allergies can develop quite suddenly, which means one day your body might like eating eggs, but the next day it might not. Always tell a grown-up if you feel funny after a meal.

The good news is that even if you are allergic to something, there'll still be lots and lots AND LOTS of other stuff you can eat that your tummy will find yummy. When Daniel Tiger can't eat the peach pie, Mom Tiger makes him banana bread muffins instead. Daniel thinks they're deee-licious and isn't sad anymore!

You can like a food but still have an allergy.

Breakfast

In Daniel Tiger's neighborhood, everyone knows that the best way to start each day is to eat a filling breakfast. In this section, you'll find lots of tasty options that will leave children feeling ready for anything. Grrrrrrrr!

Dad Tiger's Homemade Apple and Pecan Granola

Preparation time: 20 minutes • Cooking time: 3½ hours • Makes 8 servings

INGREDIENTS

2 apples, diced

2 cups (7 oz/200 g) rolled oats

1 cup (3½ oz/100 g) pecan nuts, coarsely chopped

⅓ cup (1¾ oz/50 g) pumpkin seeds

1½ teaspoons ground cinnamon

Pinch of salt (optional)

½ cup (5½ oz/160 g) honey

2 tablespoons sunflower oil

Milk or yogurt, to serve

Berries, to serve (optional)

Full of goodness, a bowl of Dad Tiger's granola is a grr-ific way to begin a day. You can buy the dried apple from the store or make your own.

1 Preheat the oven to 200°F (100°C). Line a large baking sheet with parchment paper and spread the diced apple over it. Cook the apples for 3 hours, stirring a couple of times during cooking, until dried out. Leave to cool on the baking sheet.

2 To make the granola, preheat the oven to 315°F (160°C). Put the oats, pecan nuts, pumpkin seeds, cinnamon, and salt, if using, in a large mixing bowl and mix to combine.

3 Put the honey and oil in a saucepan and set over low heat until the honey has melted and is runnier. Pour the honey mixture into the mixing bowl and mix really well until everything is coated in the honey. Tip the granola onto a large baking sheet and spread out.

4 Cook for 25 to 30 minutes, stirring occasionally, until everything is golden brown. Allow to cool undisturbed on the baking sheet, and it should clump together as it cools down. Once cool, transfer the granola to a jar to store until ready to serve. It will keep for a few weeks.

5 Serve the granola with milk or on top of yogurt, with berries, if you like.

VG If you want to make your granola vegan, simply use maple syrup instead of honey and serve with a plant milk or yogurt.

GF The granola is naturally gluten-free, but you may want to buy gluten-free oats.

DAD TIGER'S TIP:
Use red apples and leave the skins on for a really pretty pink in your granola.

Henrietta's
Raspberry and Vanilla Oatmeal

Preparation time: 5 minutes • Cooking time: 5 minutes • Makes 2 adult or 4 kid servings

INGREDIENTS

Heaped ½ cup (2¾ oz/80 g) steel-cut oats

1½ cups (12 fl. oz./350 ml) milk, plus extra, if needed

¾ cup (3½ oz/100 g) frozen raspberries, plus optional extra to serve

1 teaspoon vanilla bean paste

Katerina Kittycat loves it when her mom makes her this delicious oatmeal for breakfast. It's so yummy it tastes like dessert. Meow meow!

1 Put the oats in a saucepan and add the milk, plus the raspberries and vanilla bean paste, and mix everything together well.

2 Cook over low heat, stirring frequently, until the oats are cooked, the raspberries defrosted, and the oatmeal has thickened. Add extra milk if needed, or if you like it runnier.

3 Divide into bowls and allow to cool a little before eating. Add a few extra raspberries on top, if you like.

Good morning, neighbor, meow meow.

MOM TIGER'S TIP: This can also be made with old-fashioned rolled oats, but you will have to let it cook a little longer, adding a splash more milk or water, if needed.

18

VG If you'd like to make this dairy-free and vegan, use a plant-based milk.

GF The oatmeal is naturally gluten-free, but you may want to buy gluten-free oats.

Baby Margaret's Tropical Fruit Dippers

Preparation time: 10 minutes • Makes 4 servings

INGREDIENTS

- ½ pineapple
- 1 mango
- ¼–½ baby watermelon (or a chunk of a large one)
- Large cup of coconut yogurt
- Banana chips (optional)

This inviting tropical fruit and yogurt breakfast is easy to make and great for little ones, who will love the bright colors and refreshing taste.

1 Slice the peel off the pineapple, then slice it into fingers. Remove any tough core from the fingers. Place them on a serving plate.

2 Cut the cheeks off the mango, then slice them up into fingers. Slide a knife between the flesh and skin of each finger to remove the skin. Slice any remaining flesh from the pit and discard any skin still attached. Arrange the mango on the same serving plate as the pineapple.

3 Slice the watermelon into small wedges, with a little skin still attached to hold them by, and place on the plate, too.

4 Finally, put the coconut yogurt in a bowl and serve with the fruit. Scatter everything with banana chips, for extra tropical flavor, if you wish!

Time for breakfast, Margaret!

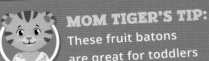

MOM TIGER'S TIP: These fruit batons are great for toddlers who are just learning to feed themselves, as their long shape makes them easier for little hands to hold.

20

Mr. McFeely's
Nutty No-Bake Breakfast Squares

Preparation time: 10 minutes • Cooking time: 10 minutes • Makes 16 squares

INGREDIENTS

- 9 ounces (250 g) soft pitted dates, chopped
- ¼ cup (2 fl. oz./60 ml) apple juice, plus a splash extra if needed
- Scant ⅔ cup (5½ oz/150 g) smooth peanut butter
- ½ cup (4 fl. oz./120 ml) maple syrup
- 5 cups (4½ oz/125 g) puffed brown rice
- 1¼ cups (5½ oz/150 g) mixed roasted nuts, roughly chopped

These nutty treats are great for breakfast on the go, which is perfect for neighborhood delivery man Mr. McFeely, who is always in a hurry. This recipe makes 16 kid-sized squares or 12 adult-sized bars.

1 Line a 9-inch (23-cm) square brownie pan with parchment paper.

2 Put dates and apple juice in a small saucepan over low heat. Stir frequently, for 6 to 7 minutes, until the dates have cooked down to a thick purée. Give them a mash with a wooden spoon to speed things along, and add a little extra apple juice if they are starting to stick to the pan.

3 Once the dates are broken down, add the peanut butter to the pan and let it melt, then add the maple syrup and stir everything together.

4 Put the puffed rice and nuts into a big bowl and pour in the sticky date and peanut mixture.

5 Carefully mix the date mixture into the rice and nuts, making sure everything is evenly coated.

6 Tip the mixture into your brownie pan and spread evenly, then press it down firmly—a flexible spatula is useful for this. Pop the tray in the fridge to chill and set for a few hours.

7 Once set, cut the block up into bars or squares with a large knife and enjoy! They will keep in the fridge for a few days.

Morning is a special time of day!

22

MOM TIGER'S TIP: Daniel likes to use a mixture of hazelnuts and walnuts in his breakfast bars.

Grandpere Tiger's
Fruity Vanilla Breakfast Waffles

INGREDIENTS

- ⅔ cup (5¾ oz/160 g) all-purpose flour
- 1 teaspoon baking powder
- 1 egg
- 1 cup (8 fl. oz./240 ml) milk
- 2 teaspoons vanilla extract
- Cooking spray
- Mixed berries, to serve
- Maple syrup, to serve

Filled with bursts of fruity flavor, children will enjoy helping to make these yummy waffles —and they'll like eating them even more.

1 Preheat the waffle maker to medium heat.

2 Sift the flour and baking powder into a bowl.

3 In a large jug or bowl, beat the egg, then add the milk and the vanilla extract and whisk everything together.

4 Pour the wet ingredients into the dry ones and whisk until you have a smooth, thick batter.

5 Once the waffle maker is hot, spritz the plates with some cooking spray to stop the waffle sticking. Pour a quarter of the batter into the machine and close the lid. Cook for about 4 minutes until the waffle is set and golden brown, then remove from the waffle maker carefully.

6 Repeat the previous step to cook three more rounds of waffles.

7 Put the waffles onto plates and pile fresh berries on top. Drizzle with maple syrup, to serve.

It's a beautiful morning in the neighborhood, Margaret!

DF If you need to make your pancakes dairy-free, just substitute the regular milk for a plant-based milk of your choice.

Dad Tiger's
Strawberry Heart Pancakes

Preparation time: 10 minutes • Cooking time: 15 minutes • Makes 4 to 6 servings

INGREDIENTS

1½ cups (200 g) all-purpose flour

2 teaspoons baking powder

Pinch of salt

2 eggs

Scant 1 cup (230 ml) milk

2¾ ounces (80 g) strawberries

Butter, for greasing

Maple syrup, for drizzling
(optional)

Equipment

Heart-shaped cookie cutter

Daniel thinks that Dad Tiger's Strawberry Heart Pancakes are deee-licious! Little ones will love mixing the pancake batter.

1 Sift the flour and baking powder into a mixing bowl and add a pinch of salt. Add the eggs and the milk and whisk everything together until you have a pancake batter with no lumps.

2 Wash the strawberries and remove the stalks, then cut the strawberries into slices. If they are big, cut the slices in half, too. Stir them gently into the pancake batter.

3 Melt a little butter in a large non-stick frying pan over medium heat and carefully rub a little more butter around the inside of a large heart-shaped cookie cutter.

4 Place the cookie cutter in the pan and spoon in enough batter to coat the surface of the pan inside the cutter. Leave to cook for about 2 minutes, until you can see bubbles appearing on the top of the pancake. Carefully remove the cookie cutter (watch out—it may be hot!), and use a spatula to flip the pancake over. Cook the other side for another minute or so until golden, then remove from the pan and keep warm while you repeat to cook the rest.

5 Serve the pancakes as they are or with a drizzle of maple syrup.

Ugga mugga, Dad!

DF If you need to make your pancakes dairy-free, just substitute the regular butter for coconut butter and milk for plant milk.

GF If you need to make them gluten-free, substitute the all-purpose flour for a gluten-free blend.

Mom Tiger's Saucy Baked Eggs

Preparation time: 10 minutes • Cooking time: 25 minutes • Makes 4 servings

INGREDIENTS

2 tablespoons olive oil

1 red onion, diced

1 garlic clove, finely chopped

2 red or orange bell peppers, sliced

2 cans (14 oz/400 g) cherry tomatoes in juice (or just use standard canned chopped tomatoes)

1 teaspoon sweet smoked paprika

Salt and pepper

4–6 eggs

Snipped chives, to sprinkle

A Tiger family favorite, these scrumptious eggs are great on weekends when you've got a little more time. You could even have them for brunch.

1 Preheat the oven to 350°F (180°C).

2 Heat the olive oil in a large frying pan with an oven-proof handle over medium heat and add the onion. Cook for 5 minutes until starting to soften. Add the garlic and the sliced bell peppers and cook for another 8 to 10 minutes until everything is really soft.

3 Add the cans of tomatoes to the pan along with the smoked paprika and stir together. Cook for another 10 minutes or so until the sauce is quite thick. Taste the sauce and add a little salt and pepper to taste.

4 Make 4 to 6 wells in the sauce with the back of a spoon and break an egg into each one. Put the pan in the preheated oven and cook for 10 minutes, or until the egg whites are cooked but the yolks are still a little runny. Leave them a little longer if you'd like the yolks cooked, too.

5 Serve the saucy eggs sprinkled with a few chives and with buttered toast on the side.

Remember to wash your hands before you start cooking.

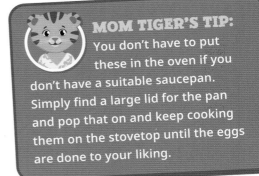

MOM TIGER'S TIP: You don't have to put these in the oven if you don't have a suitable saucepan. Simply find a large lid for the pan and pop that on and keep cooking them on the stovetop until the eggs are done to your liking.

Prince Wednesday's Breakfast Sausage Spirals

Preparation time: 2 hours • Cooking time: 25 minutes • Makes 12 spirals

INGREDIENTS

- 1 (¼ oz/7 g) packet fast-action dried yeast
- 6 tablespoons (3 fl. oz./90 ml) lukewarm water
- 1 cup plus 1 tablespoon (5½ oz/150 g) bread flour
- 1 teaspoon granulated sugar
- ½ teaspoon salt
- 2 tablespoons (1 oz/30 g) butter, melted, plus extra for brushing
- 12 breakfast sausage links

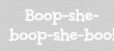

Boop-she-boop-she-boo!

These sausage snacks are royally delicious—especially dipped in ketchup or mustard. You could say they're fit for a prince!

1 Put the yeast in a jug and pour in the water. Stir together, then set aside for 5 minutes. Watch as the mixture starts to form bubbles on top!

2 Put the flour, sugar, and salt in large mixing bowl. Pour in the yeast mixture and melted butter and mix everything together until it forms into a ball of dough.

3 Tip the dough out onto a work surface and knead it for about 10 minutes. Little ones can really get into this, pounding and pulling it as they like! (Or you can use a stand mixer fitted with a dough hook.) Once it is smooth and stretchy, pop the dough into a clean bowl, cover with a warm, damp dish towel, and leave somewhere warm to proof for an hour or so, or until doubled in size.

4 Once the dough has risen, tip it onto the work surface again and knead briefly to knock out the air. Divide the dough into 12 equal portions, covering the ones you aren't using with the damp towel.

5 Take a dough portion and roll it out into a rope about 9 inches (23 cm) long by using the palms of your hands on a flat work surface.

6 Twist the dough rope around a sausage, leaving the spiral a little open. Place on a lined baking sheet and repeat with the remaining dough portions and sausages. Cover with a damp towel and leave to rise for another 30 minutes. Meanwhile, preheat the oven to 400°F (200°C).

7 Pop the tray of sausages in the oven and immediately turn the temperature down to 315°F (160°C). Bake the sausage spirals for about 25 minutes, or until golden and risen.

DAD TIGER'S TIP: If you want your sausages to be a bit crispier, quickly brown them in a pan first and let them cool before twisting the dough around them.

Fun Facts about Breakfast!

Share these tigertastic facts with your family and neighbors.

Breakfast is the first meal of the day. It is usually eaten in the morning.

The world's first breakfast cereal was created in 1863—that's more than 150 years ago!

The world's largest pancake was made in 1994 and weighed 6,614 pounds—about the same weight as a baby blue whale.

The average American eats 160 bowls of cereal a year.

More than 50 BILLION bananas are eaten at breakfast time every year.

The average strawberry has 200 seeds.

Peru has a breakfast drink made from raw fish.

Eggs are the most popular breakfast food around the world.

Learn with me!

Every day in Britain, five million people eat more than 12 million sausages. That's a lot of sausages!

The first people to eat waffles were the Ancient Greeks.

Lunch

When you're a busy parent like Mom Tiger, coming up with new ideas for lunch can be a challenge. From tasty sandwiches to delicious muffins, this section is full to bursting with healthy suggestions that children won't be able to resist.

Dad Tiger's Magnificent Cheese Sandwiches

Preparation time: 10 minutes • Makes 4 sandwiches

INGREDIENTS

- 8 slices bread
- Butter, for spreading
- 4 large lettuce leaves
- 7 ounces (200 g) sliced Cheddar cheese
- 9 ounces (250 g) coleslaw

These easy-to-make cheese sandwiches will satisfy even the hungriest tummies. Serve with apples and carrots for added goodness.

1 Lay out your slices of bread and butter them.

2 Lay a slice of lettuce onto four of the bread slices, then top the lettuce with a slice of cheese.

3 Top the cheese with a spoonful of coleslaw and spread it out carefully, then place the other four bread slices on top to make four sandwiches.

4 Cut the sandwiches in half and pop them into lunch bags to take out on your picnic!

Say cheese, Daniel.

DAD TIGER'S TIP: Pink coleslaw, made with red cabbage instead of the usual white, makes these sandwiches look extra fun and tasty!

GF If you want to make your sandwiches gluten-free, simply use a gluten-free loaf.

Queen Sara's
Lunchbox Kebobs

Preparation time: 15 minutes • Makes 8 kebobs

INGREDIENTS

8 cherry tomatoes

1 bell pepper (any color)

¼ cucumber

16 strips thick-cut ham

16 mini mozzarella balls

These cute little kebobs make lunchtime so much more fun—especially when it comes to picking the ingredients. What will you choose?

1 First, prepare your veggies. Cut the cherry tomatoes in half and dice the bell pepper into large pieces. Chop the cucumber into chunks.

2 Thread the ham, cheese, and veggies onto 8 skewers, dividing everything equally between the skewers. Try to weave the ham strips between the veggie pieces and cheese for a pretty effect.

3 Serve the skewers for lunch with bread. The skewers will keep in a sealed container in the refrigerator for 2 to 3 days.

These taste royally great with bread!

VG You can easily make these kebobs vegetarian or vegan. Replace the ham with long ribbons of cucumber or carrot, and wind them around the skewers, and use a plant-based cheese, if needed.

Baker Aker's Bean and Cheese Quesadilla Wedges

Preparation time: 10 minutes • Cooking time: 10 minutes • Makes 6 wedges

INGREDIENTS

2 tablespoons olive oil

1 (14 oz/400 g) can pinto beans, drained

½ teaspoon ground cumin

Squeeze of lime juice

Pinch of salt

2 large tortillas

½ small red onion, finely diced

1 tomato, deseeded and finely diced

½ avocado, peeled and finely diced

Scant 1 cup (2¾ oz/80 g) grated Cheddar cheese

Baker Aker loves to make quesadillas when he dances! Feeling brave? Try adding a few chili flakes when you cook the pinto beans.

1 Heat the oil in a saucepan over low heat and add the beans, cumin, lime juice, and salt. Cook for a few minutes until the beans are warm, mashing them up a little in the process so you have a rough, chunky purée.

2 Lay a tortilla on a board and spread the warm bean mixture over it. Sprinkle the onion, tomato, and avocado over the top. Finally, top with the grated cheese. Place the second tortilla on top and press down gently so everything is mushed together.

3 Slide the filled tortilla from the board into a large frying pan and place over low to medium heat. Cook for 5 minutes or so, until the base is crisp and browned. Place the board or a plate over the pan and, carefully and wearing oven mitts, flip the board and pan over to turn out the tortilla. Slide it back into the pan and cook on the other side for a few minutes until the cheese is melted.

4 Tip the tortilla back onto the board and slice into wedges to serve.

You will need a really big frying pan for this recipe!

DF **VG** If you want to make these dairy-free and vegan, simply swap the Cheddar cheese for a plant-based cheese that will melt.

MOM TIGER'S TIP: If you want to make this tasty lunch even healthier, try using whole wheat tortillas instead of white ones. It will still work grrr-eat!

Max's
Pea and Mint Frittata Muffins

Preparation time: 10 minutes • Cooking time: 20 minutes • Makes 8 muffins

INGREDIENTS

Butter, for greasing

1 cup (4½ oz/125 g) frozen peas, defrosted

2 ounces (60 g) feta cheese

4 eggs

2 tablespoons milk

Few mint leaves, finely chopped

Salt and pepper

Teacher Harriet and Max make these munchy muffins whenever he comes to visit. With eight in a batch, why not share them with your neighbors?

1 Preheat the oven to 350°F (180°C). Grease 8 holes of a muffin tray really well, then line the bases with a circle of parchment paper.

2 Divide the peas equally between the 8 lined holes, then crumble up the cheese into small pieces and divide that between the holes, too.

3 In a large jug, whisk together the eggs and milk. Add the chopped mint and season with salt and pepper. Pour the egg mixture into the holes, dividing it evenly.

4 Bake for 15 to 20 minutes until risen and golden on top. They will sink a little when they come out of the oven, but that's normal.

 DAD TIGER'S TIP: If you don't want to spend time cutting out circles of parchment paper, you can use cupcake liners to line the muffin pan holes.

Hi Max, these muffins look grr-ific.

42

Baker Aker's Savory Scones

INGREDIENTS

- ⅔ cup (3 oz/85 g) bread flour
- ⅔ cup (3 oz/85 g) all-purpose flour
- ¼ teaspoon salt
- 1 teaspoon baking powder
- 2 tablespoons (1 oz/30 g) butter, chilled and cubed
- 4 scallions, finely sliced
- ⅔ cup (2 oz/60 g) grated Cheddar cheese, plus an extra small handful to sprinkle
- ¼ cup (2 fl. oz./60 ml) milk
- 1 egg

Crumbly and filling, Baker Aker's Savory Scones are every bit as delicious as they look—and easy to make, too. Enjoy with a nice glass of cold milk.

1 Preheat oven to 400°F (200°C) and line a baking sheet with parchment paper.

2 Put flours, salt, and baking powder in a large mixing bowl and add the butter. Rub the butter into the flour with your fingertips until you have a rough, breadcrumb-like mixture, then stir in the scallions and cheese.

3 Beat the milk and egg together in a small bowl, then add this to the flour mixture. Stir with a wooden spoon until everything is mixed—you may have to switch to using your hands toward the end to make sure everything is incorporated, but be careful not to overmix or the scones may be tough.

4 Tip the dough out onto a lightly floured surface and form it into a round about 1 inch (2.5 cm) thick. Transfer it to the lined baking sheet. Use a large knife to score wedges into the dough, cutting almost all the way down to the tray.

5 Bake for about 20 minutes, or until risen and lightly golden on top. Enjoy warm or allow to cool. Best eaten the same day, or pop them in the freezer.

Won't you bake along with me?

MOM TIGER'S TIP:
If you like, you can make these bacon, cheese, and scallion scones! Just cook 4 slices of bacon until crispy, then let them cool and chop them up. Add the bacon to the scone mix along with the scallions.

Tigey
Little Bagel Pizza Faces

Preperation time: 20 minutes • Cooking time: 5 minutes • Makes 8 halves

INGREDIENTS

4 bagels, sliced in half

8 heaping teaspoons tomato paste

2 ounces (60 g) mozzarella cheese

Few pinches of dried oregano

Plus your choice of veggies to decorate:

- Halved or quartered cherry tomatoes
- Strips of bell pepper in any color
- Rings of red onion
- Sliced button mushrooms
- Halved olives

Follow this easy recipe to make your very own Tigey—and then give him some friends. This is a great way to get your little ones to eat lots of veggies.

1 Preheat the broiler. Toast the bagel halves lightly, either under the broiler or quickly in a toaster.

2 Spread the cut side of each bagel half with a heaping teaspoon of tomato paste.

3 Rip up the mozzarella into small pieces and place it onto the bagels, spreading it out evenly. Sprinkle a pinch of oregano over each bagel.

4 Now for the fun part! Use the vegetables to create faces on the bagels, using the hole in the middle as the nose. Try adding eyes and ears, as well as whiskers and tiger stripes to make the faces look like Tigey!

5 Place the bagels on a baking sheet and place under the broiler. Broil for about 5 minutes, until the veggies are softened and browning a little and the cheese is melted.

 DAD TIGER'S TIP: You don't just have to use the toppings suggested here—you could add ham, pineapple, corn, anchovies ... anything you fancy! Or try switching out the mozzarella for Cheddar or even goat's cheese. Have fun with what you have!

DF Make these dairy-free and vegan by using a plant-based cheese.

VG

GF If you need to make these gluten-free, just use gluten-free bagels.

O the Owl's
Rice Paper Shrimp Rolls

Preparation time: 20 minutes • Makes 12 rolls

INGREDIENTS

- 1 nest (about 1¾ oz/50 g) rice vermicelli noodles
- 1 carrot, peeled and cut into thin strips
- ¼ cucumber, cut into thin strips
- 4 large scallions, shredded into thin strips
- Small bunch of mint leaves
- Small bunch of Thai basil or cilantro leaves
- 24 cooked jumbo shrimp
- Sweet chili sauce, for dipping
- 12 rice spring roll wrappers

Children will have a great time stuffing these yummy rolls. If they're brave enough, they could try dunking them in the sweet chili dip.

1 Put the noodles in a bowl and pour boiling water over them. Leave them to soak for 5 minutes until tender, then drain the noodles well and transfer to another bowl.

2 Lay all the vegetables out in bowls on the dining table. Put the herbs in another bowl and the shrimp in a bowl, too. Put a small bowl of sweet chili sauce on the table, as well as a stack of the rice papers.

3 Put a shallow bowl of hand-hot water on the table for soaking the rice paper discs.

4 To make your own shrimp rolls, place a rice paper wrapper into the water for a few seconds. Put it on your plate, then fill it with a little pile of noodles, a few veggies, a couple of shrimp, and a few herb leaves, arranging it all in a little sausage shape horizontally in the middle. Fold over the sides of the disc to cover the ends of your sausage, then fold the bottom over and continue to roll it all up like a mini burrito. Enjoy dipped into the chili sauce, if you dare!

> These rolls are nifty galifty!

VG If you want to make these vegan, just switch the shrimp for tofu, or leave them out entirely.

MOM TIGER'S TIP:
These can be easily
adapted to what you have.
If you don't have shrimp, you could
use some cooked chicken or tofu.
They will all be delicious dipped into
yummy sweet chili sauce!

Teddy and Leo Platypus's
Favorite Pesto Pinwheels

Preparation time: 10 minutes • Cooking time: 20 minutes • Makes 8 pinwheels

INGREDIENTS

- 1 sheet ready-rolled puff pastry
- 3 ounces (80 g) pesto (fresh is best, but use jarred if you can't find that)

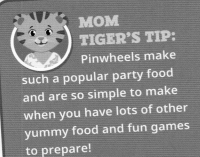

MOM TIGER'S TIP: Pinwheels make such a popular party food and are so simple to make when you have lots of other yummy food and fun games to prepare!

Teddy and Leo Platypus like making these with their big sister, Jodi. With only two ingredients, this is a great starter recipe for young children.

1 Preheat the oven to 400°F (200°C) and line a baking sheet with parchment paper.

2 Unroll the pastry, keeping it on its sheet of parchment paper—this is useful to help you roll it up again later. Spread the pesto over the pastry sheet, leaving a ½-inch (1cm) strip along one of the short ends bare of pesto.

3 Starting at the other short end (where the pesto does go right to the edge), roll up the pastry street as you would a jelly roll. Dampen the bare strip with a little water and seal, then turn the roll over so the sealed edge is in the bottom.

4 Slice the roll into 12 pieces, then lay them, cut sides up, on the prepared baking sheet.

5 Bake the pinwheels for 18 to 20 minutes, until light golden and puffed up.

Would you like to play hide-and-seek with us?

DF
VG Most store-bought puff pastry is vegan (but check the label) and you can buy vegan pesto without the Parmesan cheese.

GF If you need to make them gluten-free, use a gluten-free puff pastry.

Grandpere Tiger's Potato and Pickle Salad

Preparation time: 10 minutes • Cooking time: 20 minutes • Serves a family of 4

INGREDIENTS

- 1 pound 9 ounces (700 g) potatoes
- 5 tablespoons mayonnaise
- 1 teaspoon mustard, such as French's
- 2 ounces (60 g) dill pickles (about 2 pickles), drained and finely diced
- Snipped chives, to serve (optional)

Kids will love all the different colors and surprising flavors in this scrumptious salad. Serve with juicy tomatoes and crispy lettuce.

1 Place a large pot of water over high heat and bring it to a boil while you peel the potatoes and cut them into large chunks.

2 Add the potatoes to the boiling water and cook for about 20 minutes, or until tender when pierced with a fork. Drain and leave to steam-dry and cool a little in the colander for a couple of minutes.

3 Meanwhile, mix the mayonnaise, mustard, and pickles together in a large bowl.

4 Once cool, tip the potatoes into the bowl with the dressing and stir everything together. Sprinkle with snipped chives to serve, if you like.

Cooking with Grandpere is fun!

VG Use a plant-based mayonnaise to make this salad vegan.

DAD TIGER'S TIP:
Grandpere's pickles are also great sliced and added to burgers—try adding pickles to Prince Tuesday's Super Sliders on page 68.

Dinner

After a busy day of work and play, there's nothing nicer than sitting down with your family to enjoy a hearty dinner. In this section, you'll find lots of grr-ific options for evening meals, from chicken tacos to campfire stew. Most of these recipes are designed to serve a family of four, but if you double the ingredients, you'll have enough to invite your neighbors.

Miss Elaina's Veggie Spaghetti Dinner

Preparation time: 20 minutes • Cooking time: 40 minutes • Serves a family of 4

INGREDIENTS

1 red onion, sliced into thin wedges

2 red bell peppers, seeded and chopped into large dice

1 butternut squash, seeded and diced

1 eggplant, diced

1 zucchini, diced

3–4 tablespoons olive oil

Salt and pepper

About 8 ounces (225 g) dried spaghetti pasta

1 ounce (30 g) Parmesan cheese, finely grated, plus extra to serve

Small handful of fresh oregano leaves

This veggie-packed dish is fun to make and even more fun to eat. Best served with bibs (for both kids and adults)—spaghetti can get brilliantly messy!

1 Preheat the oven to 375°F (190°C). Once you have chopped your veggies, spread them out over two lipped baking sheets.

2 Drizzle your vegetables generously with the oil and season with a little salt and pepper, then stir to make sure they are coated. Bake the veggies for about 40 minutes, stirring occasionally, until everything is really soft and caramelizing on the edges.

3 When the vegetables have 10 minutes left, start cooking the pasta in a large pan of boiling water as per the package instructions. Once cooked, drain and tip back into the warm saucepan.

4 Scrape the cooked vegetables from the baking sheets into the pan of spaghetti and stir everything together. Don't worry if the vegetables break up a bit as you stir.

5 Add the Parmesan and oregano leaves to the pan and stir again. Add a bit more seasoning, too, if you like.

6 Serve the veggie spaghetti in pasta bowls with a little more cheese and a few more leaves sprinkled over the top.

If it's Backward Day, you can have this for breakfast!

DF To make this dish dairy-free and vegan, use a plant-based cheese, or just leave the cheese out.

GF You can buy good varieties of gluten-free pasta if standard spaghetti is off the table.

O the Owl's Cheesy Parsnip Nuggets

Preparation time: 20 minutes • Cooking time: 25 minutes • Makes 12 nuggets

INGREDIENTS

Cooking oil spray

1 pound 2 ounces (500 g) parsnips, peeled and grated

Heaped 1 cup (3½ oz/100 g) grated Cheddar cheese

1 teaspoon dried thyme

3 tablespoons all-purpose flour

⅔ cup (1 oz/30 g) panko breadcrumbs

Hoo hoo! O the Owl's cheesy nuggets are melt-in-your-mouth delicious and a great idea for getting kids to try lots of new vegetables.

1 Preheat the oven to 350°F (180°C) and lightly grease a baking sheet with a little cooking spray.

2 Put the grated parsnips in a microwaveable bowl and cover with a plate. Pop in the microwave on high power for 3 minutes to soften and partly cook them.

3 To the bowl with the cooked parsnip, add the grated cheese and thyme and carefully mix it all together. The hot parsnip will probably melt the cheese a little, but that's okay, as it will help it all bind together and also help the crumbs to stick. Now add the flour and briefly mix that in, too.

4 Tip the panko crumbs onto a plate. While still warm, but not too hot for little hands, scoop a large walnut-size ball of the parsnip mix and roll into a ball. Flatten it a little into a patty shape, then roll it in the crumbs until they are stuck all over the surface and it is completely covered. Place it on the greased baking sheet and repeat to make the rest of the nuggets—you should be able to make about 12.

5 Pop them in the oven and bake for 15 minutes, then take them out and turn them over with a spatula. Return to the oven and bake for another 10 minutes, or until crisp and golden all over.

> It's fun to try new things, hoo hoo!

 If you want to make these gluten-free, use flour and dried breadcrumbs that are gluten-free.

The Tigers' Family Veggie Campfire Stew

Preparation time: 10 minutes • Cooking time: 35 minutes • Serves a family of 4

INGREDIENTS

2 tablespoons olive oil

1 onion, diced

7 ounces (200 g) mushrooms, sliced

1 medium–large sweet potato (about 9 oz/250 g), peeled and diced

1 red bell pepper, seeded and chopped into large dice

1 garlic clove, finely chopped

1¾ cups (14 fl. oz./400 ml) vegetable stock

1 (5 oz/425 g) can diced tomatoes

1 tablespoon tomato paste

2 teaspoons dried mixed herbs

1 (5 oz/425 g) can cannellini beans, drained and rinsed

Salt and pepper

Crusty bread, to serve

All it takes to make this Tiger Family favorite is a few simple veggies and pantry ingredients. And don't forget crusty bread to dunk in it!

1 Heat the oil in a large pan and add the onion. Cook over low–medium heat for 5 minutes until the onion is slightly softened. Add the mushrooms to the pan and cook with the onions for another 5 minutes.

2 Add the sweet potato and bell pepper to the pan and cook for another 3 minutes until slightly softened, then add the garlic.

3 Pour in the stock and chopped tomatoes, then add the tomato paste, dried herbs, and cannellini beans. Cook for about 20 minutes, until all the veggies have softened.

4 Taste the stew and add salt and pepper to your taste, then serve with crusty bread.

 MOM TIGER'S TIP: Make this simple one-pot stew over your campfire or in your kitchen—it will still be just as delicious!

This stew tastes amazing!

Dr. Anna's
Coconut Dhal

Preperation time: 10 minutes • Cooking time: 30 minutes • Serves a family of 4

INGREDIENTS

1 tablespoon coconut oil
(or cooking oil)

1 onion, finely diced

1 tablespoon garlic paste

1 teaspoon ginger paste

1 teaspoon ground cumin

1 teaspoon ground coriander

1 vegetable stock cube

2½ cups (600 ml) boiling water

1 cup (250 g) red lentils

1 (14 oz/400 g) can coconut
milk

Salt

Juice of 1 lime

Large handful of cilantro,
coarsely chopped

Little ones will love Dr. Anna's yummy mild dhal. The delicious sweetness of the coconut makes it more accessible for new tasters.

1 Melt the coconut oil in a large saucepan over low–medium heat and add the onion. Cook for a good 6 to 7 minutes, until tender, then add the garlic and ginger pastes and the ground spices and cook for a further 1 minute.

2 Dissolve the stock cube in the boiling water and add it to the pan along with the lentils and coconut milk. Cook for 15 to 20 minutes, or until the lentils are tender, stirring very frequently, as the lentils have a habit of sticking to the bottom of the pan. If it is becoming too dry, add a splash more hot water.

3 Once the lentils are cooked, season to taste with salt and stir in the lime juice and most of the cilantro.

4 Serve the dhal sprinkled with the remaining cilantro.

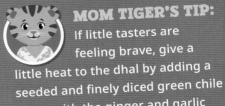

MOM TIGER'S TIP: If little tasters are feeling brave, give a little heat to the dhal by adding a seeded and finely diced green chile along with the ginger and garlic pastes. It still won't be too hot.

The Platypus Family's Pan Pans

Preparation time: 30 minutes • Cooking time: 45 minutes • Makes 8 pan pans

INGREDIENTS

- 2 tablespoons olive oil
- 7 ounces (200 g) potatoes, peeled and finely diced
- 1 carrot (about 3½ oz/100 g), peeled and finely diced
- ¼ small cabbage, shredded (about 4 oz/120 g)
- 6 scallions, sliced
- 1 teaspoon sweet smoked paprika
- 1 teaspoon dried thyme
- 3 tablespoons water
- Salt and pepper
- 2 sheets ready-rolled pie dough
- 1 egg, beaten

Add some fun to your evening meal by serving dinner in parcels. Full to bursting with veggies, these pastries will be gone before you know it.

1 Heat the oil in a sauté pan or large frying pan with a lid over medium heat and add the potatoes and carrot. Cook for about 8 minutes until the veggies are softening and picking up a little color.

2 Add the cabbage and the scallions to the pan, along with the paprika, thyme, and water. Stir in, then pop the lid on the pan and cook for about 8 minutes until all the cabbage is wilted down. Make sure you stir occasionally so the veggies don't burn. Season with salt and pepper, then let cool completely.

3 Preheat the oven to 350°F (180°C) and line a baking sheet with parchment paper.

4 Unroll the pie dough sheets and use a 5-inch (13-cm) cookie cutter to stamp out 8 circles from the pie sheets.

5 Using a pastry brush, brush the entire edge of each dough circle with a little beaten egg. Spoon some of the filling into the middle of the circle and fold one side of the circle over to make a half-moon shape. Crimp the edges together with your fingers to seal.

6 Transfer the pan pans to the lined baking sheet and brush the tops with beaten egg. Use a skewer or knife to make a couple of small holes in the top of each one to let the steam escape when cooking.

7 Bake for 20 to 25 minutes, until golden brown and puffed up.

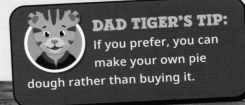

DAD TIGER'S TIP:
If you prefer, you can make your own pie dough rather than buying it.

VG If you'd like to make these vegan, use a vegan pie dough and glaze them with plant-based milk instead of egg.

GF To make these gluten-free, use a gluten-free pie dough.

Jodi's Chicken Tacos

Preparation time: 15 minutes • Cooking time: 15 minutes • Serves a family of 4

INGREDIENTS

- 1–2 teaspoons taco seasoning mix
- 14 ounces (400 g) chicken breast fillets or mini fillets, cut into chunky strips
- 2 tablespoons olive oil
- 1 red onion, sliced
- 1 red bell pepper, seeded and sliced
- 1 green bell pepper, seeded and sliced
- 1 large avocado
- Juice of ½ lime
- 8–10 soft corn tacos
- Few iceberg or Bibb lettuce leaves, shredded
- Sour cream, to serve (optional)

In need of a quick dinner idea that's hearty, fun, and filling? Jodi's chicken tacos are just the thing—they're speedy to make and yummy, too.

1 Sprinkle the taco seasoning over the chicken and mix so the chicken is all coated. Don't forget to wash your hands well after handling raw chicken!

2 Heat 1 tablespoon of the oil in a large non-stick frying pan over medium–high heat and cook the chicken for 6 to 7 minutes, or until dark golden on the outside and cooked through. (Make sure you check carefully to make sure there is no pink in the meat.) Remove the chicken from the pan and set aside.

3 Turn the heat down to medium and drizzle the remaining oil into the pan. Add the onion and cook for a couple of minutes before adding the peppers. Cook everything together for a good 7 to 8 minutes until tender and picking up some color.

4 Meanwhile, halve the avocado and remove the pit. Peel and coarsely chop the flesh and put it in a bowl. Mash it with a fork to a chunky purée, then stir in the lime juice.

5 Warm the tacos and place them on a plate on the dining table. Put the chicken pieces on another plate, and the pepper and onion mix on a third plate. Put the bowl of mashed avocado on the table, too, along with a bowl of shredded lettuce.

6 Let everyone dig in and assemble their own tacos, adding a bit of lettuce, chicken, peppers, and onion, and then a dollop of avocado on top! Drizzle with sour cream, too, if you like.

Yippy skippy!

VG To make these vegan, use a meat substitute product, such as seitan or tofu, in place of the chicken and skip the sour cream.

GF Use 100% corn tacos if you need to make these gluten-free.

DAD TIGER'S TIP:
You could also have salmon in your tacos—use the recipe for Baby Margaret's Salmon Fish Sticks on page 70 and stuff your tacos with these and salad leaves or coleslaw.

Prince Tuesday's Super Sliders

Preparation time: 20 minutes • Cooking time: 5 minutes • Makes 10 sliders

INGREDIENTS

10 ounces (300 g) ground beef

Salt and pepper

Drizzle of oil

10 mini brioche buns

Mayonnaise, for spreading

Few lettuce leaves

Several thin slices of cheese (such as mild Cheddar)

Red onion rings

Few small tomatoes, sliced

Royally recommended by Prince Tuesday, these tiny burgers are perfect for a treat-night dinner. Serve with a drizzle of your favorite condiment.

1 Season the beef lightly and divide into 10 equal portions, each about an ounce (30 g). Shape each portion into a patty by rolling it into a ball in your palms and then flattening it. Don't forget to wash your hands well after handling raw meat!

2 Heat a drizzle of oil in a large non-stick frying pan over medium heat and add the patties to the pan. Cook for about 5 minutes, turning over halfway through cooking, until they are browned on the outside and cooked all the way through.

3 Now for the fun part of assembling your burgers! Slice a bun in half and spread a little mayonnaise on the bottom half. Add a lettuce leaf, then a warm burger, followed by a slice of cheese. Top the cheese with a slice of onion and a slice of tomato. Place the top of the burger bun on the very top. If you like, you could pop a skewer through it all to hold it together.

Extra cheese for me, please!

DF If you want to make these dairy-free, skip the cheese or use a dairy-free variety.

GF To make these gluten-free, just use gluten-free buns.

68

Baby Margaret's Salmon Fish Sticks

Preparation time: 20 minutes • Cooking time: 10 minutes • Serves a family of 4

INGREDIENTS

Few tablespoons all-purpose flour

2 eggs, beaten

1 cup (1¾ oz/50 g) panko breadcrumbs

3–4 thick salmon fillets

3 tablespoons oil, for frying

These finger-licking fish sticks are great for little ones like Baby Margaret as they're soft to eat and nutritious. For bigger kids, serve with delish salad.

1 Set up a production line: put the flour onto a plate, and the beaten eggs and breadcrumbs each into a shallow bowl. Cut your salmon fillets into thick strips.

2 Dip the salmon strips first into the flour and shake off the excess, then into the beaten egg, then into the breadcrumbs, making sure they are completely coated. Place them on a baking sheet.

3 Heat the oil in a large non-stick frying pan and fry the fish sticks for a few minutes on each side until golden brown all over and the fish is opaque and cooked all the way through.

These fish sticks are yummy in our tummies!

DAD TIGER'S TIP: If you would like to make these fish sticks even more healthy, you can bake them instead of frying—just pop them on a lined baking sheet in an oven preheated to 350°F (180°C) for about 25 minutes, or until the crumbs are browning and the fish is cooked through.

GF If you need to make your fish sticks gluten-free, just substitute the panko crumbs for a gluten-free variety of dried breadcrumbs.

Amira's
Rainbow Tuna Sweet Potatoes

Preparation time: 15 minutes • Cooking time: 45 minutes • Serves a family of 4

INGREDIENTS

- 4 (or more if they are smaller) sweet potatoes (select the sizes most suitable for your family)
- ½ red bell pepper, seeded and diced
- ½ orange bell pepper, seeded and diced
- 4-inch (10-cm) chunk cucumber, diced
- 3 scallions, finely sliced
- 1 (7 oz/200 g) can whole kernel corn, drained
- 2 (5 oz/140 g) cans tuna
- ⅔ cup (5½ oz/150 g) thick, Greek-style yogurt
- Salt and pepper

This fun dinner has all the colors of the rainbow and is yummy, too. Brightly colored fruit and veggies mean there are lots of vitamins in them.

1 Preheat the oven to 350°F (180°C).

2 Put the potatoes in the oven and bake for about 30 minutes until soft. Any larger potatoes may need an extra 10 to 15 minutes.

3 Meanwhile, prepare all of your veggies and put them in a large bowl.

4 Drain the cans of tuna and add them to the bowl, then stir in the Greek yogurt. Add a little salt and pepper to taste.

5 Once the potatoes are cooked and soft, put them onto serving plates and cut them in half.

6 Pile the tuna filling into the potatoes and serve.

I like making these potatoes with my little brother, Max.

MOM TIGER'S TIP: You don't have to use the exact veggies here ... if you don't like scallions, add sliced celery; if peppers aren't your thing, try quartered cherry tomatoes. Adapt to what you have in your refrigerator!

DF To make this dairy-free, you could use mayonnaise instead of yogurt.

Dinnertime Look & Find!

Daniel Tiger is helping Mom Tiger make dinner in the kitchen. Look closely at this picture. **How many carrots can you spot?**

CAN YOU ALSO FIND...?

Salt and Pepper

Bell Pepper

Fork

Banana

Tigey

Turn to page 127 for the answers!

Snacks and Drinks

When it comes to planning mealtimes, it's easy to forget about snacks and drinks but they're a great way of keeping children's energy levels topped up throughout the day. In this section, you'll find lots of healthy options that are not only easy to make and full of fruit and veggie goodness, but will spark imaginations, too.

Katerina Kittycat's Ladybug Treats

INGREDIENTS

- 2 red apples, washed well
- 2 tablespoons smooth peanut butter
- Small handful of raisins
- Pretzel sticks

These little apple ladybugs are almost too cute to eat. For extra kitchen fun, count out loud as you add the raisins—how high can you go?

1 To make the ladybug shape, cut the cheek off of an apple, leaving behind the core. Turn the apple around and cut the cheek off the other side so you have two rounded discs.

2 Now cut a long, thin triangle shape out of the bottom edge of each apple disc—this will make it look like it has wings.

3 Use a teaspoon and your fingers to add small blobs of peanut butter all over the apples. Try and spread them out and leave space between them. Put a large splodge of peanut butter at the top of the circle, on the opposite side to the cut you have made.

4 Place a raisin onto each of the blobs of peanut butter to make the spots on a ladybug's wings. Put two raisins in the middle of the large spot of peanut butter to make the ladybug's eyes.

5 Finally, stick a short pretzel stick on either side of the eyes to make the antennae.

Count the spots with me, meow-meow!

MOM TIGER'S TIP: Don't let the rest of the apple go to waste! Use it in Dad Tiger's Homemade Apple and Pecan Granola on page 16.

Daniel Tiger's Fruit Smoothie Pops

Preparation time: 20 minutes, plus freezing • Makes 6 popsicles

INGREDIENTS

1 large banana

7 ounces (200g) strawberries

Scant ½ cup (3½ fl. oz./100 ml) orange juice

Equipment

6 small disposable cups or popsicle molds

There's nothing nicer than a cold treat on a hot summer's day and these thirst-quenching pops are made from entirely natural ingredients.

1 Peel the banana and put it in a blender or food processor, breaking it into chunks as you go.

2 Wash the strawberries and remove the stalks. Halve them, or quarter them if large, and pop them in the blender with the banana.

3 Now add the orange juice and press the button on the blender to blend it all up into a thick liquid.

4 Carefully pour the liquid into the cups, dividing it evenly between them, and place them in the freezer. Set the timer for 1 hour.

5 Once the timer goes off, take the ice treats out of the freezer and add a popsicle stick to each cup, standing it up straight. Return them to the freezer until frozen solid, then enjoy!

Strawberries are my favorite fruit!

MOM TIGER'S TIP: You could also make these in layered colors! Simply blend the banana with half the orange juice, and pour that into cups to half-fill them. Let them freeze, then blend the strawberries with the remaining orange juice and pour that on top and freeze.

Mom Tiger's Fruit Skewers

Preparation time: 20 minutes • Makes as many as you'd like

INGREDIENTS

Small fruit of your choice, such as:

- Strawberries
- Blueberries
- Grapes
- Cherries, pitted
- Tangerines

Why don't you do as Mom Tiger does and serve these fruity skewers to your family in a fun watermelon bowl? See our tip below for how...

1 Prepare all your fruit; wash it well and pop it in bowls. Peel and segment the tangerines and halve any other larger fruit, such as strawberries.

2 Thread your fruit onto skewers, alternating different fruits.

3 Arrange the fruit skewers in your watermelon bowl.

That looks yummy, Mom!

MOM TIGER'S TIP: To make a watermelon bowl, cut the top two quarters off a watermelon, leaving a thick strip in the middle for the handle. Scoop out all of the pink flesh to create your bowl. You can use the flesh for King Friday's Watermelon Punch on page 92, or thread chunks of watermelon onto the skewers.

Teacher Harriet's Veggie Taster Sticks and Dip

Preparation time: 20 minutes • Makes 1 large platter

INGREDIENTS

For the hummus dip:

1 (15 oz/400 g) can chickpeas, drained

2 tablespoons tahini

1 garlic clove, finely chopped

2 tablespoons lemon juice

4 tablespoons olive oil

Pinch of ground cumin

Good pinch of salt

A selection of veggies of your choice, such as:

- Carrots, peeled and cut into strips
- Radishes (long ones work best for dipping)
- Cucumber, cut into strips
- Bell peppers, seeded and cut into strips
- Celery, cut into strips

As Teacher Harriet knows, these sticks and dip are the perfect school snack, providing a boost of natural energy that will last until hometime.

1 To make the dip, put the chickpeas into a food processor and add all the remaining ingredients. Press the button and blend everything together until smooth. (Adults may have to stop the food processor and scrape down the sides with a spatula a couple of times during blending.)

2 Chop up all your veggies into strips or other shapes that are easy to hold and dip.

3 Put the dip in a bowl and the veggies onto a plate and serve. Make sure you try all the different veggies on offer!

Will you be my helpers today?

DAD TIGER'S TIP: If you don't enjoy this dip, you could make another to go with the veggies, such as guacamole or cream cheese and chives. Try to include something you haven't tried before!

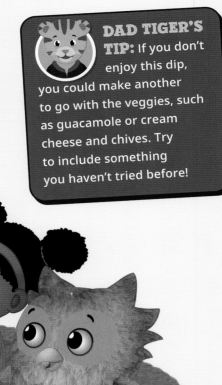

Dad Tiger's Spooky Tea Eggs

Preparation time: 10 minutes • Cooking time: 1 hour • Makes 6 eggs

INGREDIENTS

6 eggs

2 black tea bags

4 tablespoons dark soy sauce

2 teaspoons Chinese five-spice powder

2½ cups (21 fl. oz./600 ml) water

An egg-cellent recipe for encouraging kids to cook—they'll love peeling the shells to reveal the beautiful patterns underneath, which look a bit like spooky spider webs!

1 Bring a pan of water to a boil, then add the eggs. Set a timer for 5 minutes and let them cook, then immediately put the pan in the sink and run cold water into the pan to cool them. Leave the eggs in the water until completely cold.

2 Put the soy sauce, tea bags, and five-spice powder into a small saucepan with the water. Bring the water to a simmer and let the tea brew for 10 minutes or so while you prepare the eggs.

3 Once the eggs are cold, hold 1 egg in your hand and use a teaspoon to make firm taps all over the egg. This will crack the shell and create places where the dark-colored water can enter and make patterns on the egg.

4 Remove the tea bags and carefully place the cracked eggs in the simmering water (it should just cover them—if not, add more boiling water) and simmer for 30 minutes. After this time, turn the heat off and let the eggs marinate for another hour while the water cools down.

5 Now for the fun part! Drain the eggs and carefully peel off the shells to reveal the pretty patterns left on the eggs.

Did you know that eggs are full of protein, which helps you grow?

Grandpere Tiger's Favorite Raisin Bread

Preparation time: 20 minutes • Cooking time: 45 minutes • Makes 1 small loaf

INGREDIENTS

- 1½ cups (7 oz/200 g) raisins or other mixed dried fruit
- ⅔ cup (5¼ fl. oz./160 ml) boiling water
- ½ cup packed (3½ oz/100 g) dark brown sugar
- 1 egg, beaten
- 1 cup (4½ oz/130 g) self-rising flour
- ½ teaspoon baking powder
- 1 teaspoon apple pie spice

Daniel and Grandpere Tiger always have a great time making raisin bread together—now it's your turn to try. All together now: "Mixa, mixa, mixa!"

1 Grease a 1-pound loaf pan and line with parchment paper.

2 Put the raisins in a bowl and pour in the water. Leave to cool and soak for 2 to 3 hours. Toward the end of the soaking time, preheat the oven to 350°F (180°C).

3 Add the sugar to the fruit and stir in until dissolved, then beat in the egg. Sift the flour, baking powder, and apple pie spice into the bowl and fold everything together.

4 Pour the batter into the prepared pan and bake for 45 minutes, or until risen and a skewer inserted into the center of the loaf comes out clean. Leave to rest for 5 minutes in the pan, then transfer to a wire rack to cool completely.

5 To serve, slice the loaf and serve as is or spread with butter.

Remember to go slow when you stir.

VG If you would like to make this bread vegan, replace the egg with an egg substitute product.

MOM TIGER'S TIP: This bread is also yummy toasted. Simply cut into slices and pop them in the toaster, then spread with butter and enjoy.

Dr. Anna's Lassi

Preparation time: 5 minutes • Makes 2-4 servings

INGREDIENTS

- 2 cups (500 g) plain yogurt
- 1 cup (8 fl. oz./250 ml) whole milk
- 2 tablespoons granulated sugar
- ½ teaspoon ground cardamom (optional)
- Ice cubes, to serve

Did you know lassi is a popular drink in India? Enjoy Dr. Anna's version with a smile!

1 Put the yogurt, milk, sugar, and cardamom, if using, in a blender, and blend until everything is well combined.

2 Put some ice cubes in your glasses and add the lassi. Enjoy very cold.

This is a cooling drink after a day of fun!

VG You can easily make a vegan version of this lassi, too—just make sure your yogurt and milk are plant-based.

DAD TIGER'S TIP: I love serving these to my little ones in mini milk bottles with fun paper straws. Of course, reusable straws are great, too!

King Friday's Watermelon Punch

Preparation time: 5 minutes • Makes 4 servings

INGREDIENTS

½ baby watermelon, or ¼ large one, chilled

1¾–2 cups (14-17 fl. oz./ 400–500 ml) lemonade, chilled

MOM TIGER'S TIP: You don't have to use watermelon for this—lots of types of blended fruit are great for making simple lemonade more exciting, especially berries! Try it with puréed strawberries, raspberries, or blackberries.

This colorful, fruity drink is great for birthday parties, warm summer days, and important royal engagements. Let the slurping commence...

1 Slice the peel off of the watermelon and pop the flesh into a blender or food processor. Blend to a smooth purée.

2 Put a fine-mesh strainer over a large jug and pour the watermelon pulp into it. Let the juice drain through into the jug—you should get around 2 cups.

3 Pour in the lemonade to top up.

4 Divide the drink between glasses and enjoy!

A royal hello from me!

92

Music Man Stan's
Strawberry and Vanilla Shake

Preparation time: 5 minutes • Makes 4 small glasses

INGREDIENTS

- 10½ ounces (300 g) strawberries
- 6 ounces (175 g) really good vanilla ice cream
- ⅔ cup (5¼ fl. oz./160 ml) milk

Do something nice for your neighbor and make them one of these yummy shakes. Packed with real strawberries, it'll turn any frown upside down.

1 Wash the strawberries well and remove any stalks.

2 Put everything into a blender and blend until smooth, thick, and frothy.

3 Pour into glasses and enjoy!

Wowweee! This recipe makes me want to sing!

DF **VG** Feel free to use plant-based milk and ice cream to make these dairy-free and vegan.

Dad Tiger's Special Homemade Hot Chocolate

Preparation time: 5 minutes • Cooking time: 5 minutes • Makes 4 small mugs

INGREDIENTS

2½ cups (21 fl. oz./600 ml) whole milk

3½ ounces (100 g) semi-sweet or bittersweet chocolate, broken into pieces (or use good-quality chips)

Whipped cream and sprinkles or marshmallows, to serve (optional)

Dad Tiger's Special Homemade Hot Chocolate is just the thing for warming up on a cold day or as a bedtime treat. Kids will love adding the toppings.

1 Put the milk in a saucepan and add the chocolate.

2 Heat over medium heat on the stovetop, stirring frequently, until the milk is hot (but not boiling) and the chocolate has all melted.

3 Pour the hot chocolate into mugs to serve, topped with whipped cream and sprinkles or marshmallows for an extra treat.

Lots of marshmallows for me, please, Dad!

DF You can make this dairy-free by using a plant-based milk and making sure you use a high cocoa solids chocolate without added milk. Also skip the whipped cream and go for delish marshmallows!

VE Do the above and make sure you buy vegan marshmallows, too!

DAD TIGER'S TIP:
Bittersweet chocolate makes a lovely rich hot chocolate, but you may need to add a little extra sweetener as this type of chocolate tends to have less sugar in it.

Sweet Things

Make family mealtimes even more enjoyable by ending them with a deee-licious dessert. This section is filled with recipes that will make children go "mmmm!," from apple and berry crumble cups to trolley cookies—just like the ones Baker Aker makes.

Mom Tiger's Banana Swirl

Preparation time: 5 minutes, plus freezing • Makes 3-4 servings

INGREDIENTS

2 large, ripe bananas

Banana chips, nuts, or chocolate chips, to sprinkle (optional)

Children will go bananas for Mom Tiger's swirly, whirly dessert, which looks like ice cream but is made entirely from fruit.

1 The day before you would like to make the banana swirl, peel the bananas and slice them. Place them on a tray in the freezer to freeze solid.

2 To prepare the swirl, put the frozen bananas into a food processor or blender and blend until they are smooth. (An adult may need to stop the machine from time to time and scrape down the sides of the bowl to make sure it is all blended.)

3 Serve the banana swirl in bowls. If you like, you can decorate your bowls with dried banana chips, nuts, or even chocolate chips for a real treat.

What words rhyme with swirl?

DF **VG** Yummy bananas can be eaten by almost everyone, but if you follow a vegan or dairy-free diet and want to add chocolate chips, just make sure they don't have any dairy milk or milk derivatives in them.

MOM TIGER'S TIP: Make sure you put your bananas in the freezer well in advance of preparing this —they need to be very cold and frozen hard! Overnight is best.

Prince Wednesday's Apple and Berry Crumble Cups

Preparation time: 20 minutes • Cooking time: 25 minutes • Makes 4 servings

INGREDIENTS

1 large apple, cored and diced

5½–7 ounces (150–200 g) mixed berries, fresh or frozen or a mixture

¾ cup (3½ oz/100 g) all-purpose flour

¼ cup (½ stick/60 g) butter, cold and diced

5 tablespoons (2 oz/60 g) granulated sugar

These melt-in-your-mouth crumble cups are a scrumptious way to end any meal, but they will leave you with a dilemma: custard or ice cream?

1 Preheat the oven to 375°F (190°C).

2 Divide the chopped apple equally between four small ovenproof bowls or cups. Add the berries and mix them up.

3 Put the flour in a mixing bowl and add the butter. Using the tips of your fingers, rub the butter into the flour until it looks like breadcrumbs, then stir in the sugar.

4 Sprinkle the crumble mixture over the fruit in the cups. If you squeeze it in your hands as you go, some of it will clump together and give you lovely lumps of crumble.

5 Place the small dishes on a baking sheet and place in the oven for about 25 minutes, until the crumble is golden on top, the fruit is cooked, and the juice is bubbling up the sides. Make sure you let them cool down a bit before you dig in!

One crumble cup for me, one crumble cup for you!

VG **GF** **DF** You can easily make these gluten-free by using a gluten-free all-purpose flour, or substitute the butter for a plant-based spread to make them vegan and dairy free.

Katerina Kittycat's Berry Surprise

Preparation time: 5 minutes, plus setting • Makes 4-6 servings

INGREDIENTS

- 1 packet black cherry, raspberry, or cranberry flavored gelatin
- 2¼ cups (10½ oz/300 g) mixed berries, such as raspberries, blueberries, and blackberries

Berries, such as the ones in this dessert, are full of powerful antioxidants that are good for you. They are also delicious to eat!

1 Put the gelatin powder into a jug and dissolve it in hot water according to the packet instructions.

2 Put the berries into a pretty serving bowl. Pour the gelatin liquid into the bowl to cover the berries.

3 Carefully transfer the bowl to the fridge and let chill until completely set, then serve.

We love surprises!

VG If you follow a vegan diet, swap the gelatin for an alternative such as agar-agar.

Daniel Tiger's (Peach-Free) Banana Bread Muffins

Preparation time: 20 minutes • Cooking time: 20 minutes • Makes 12 muffins

INGREDIENTS

3 bananas

½ cup plus 2 tablespoons (4½ oz/120 g) packed brown sugar

2 teaspoons vanilla extract

2 eggs, beaten

7 tablespoons (3½ fl. oz./ 100 ml) sunflower oil

1⅔ cups (8 oz/225 g) whole wheat flour

1½ teaspoons baking powder

½ teaspoon baking soda

Turbinado (demerara) sugar, to sprinkle

Always check the ingredients before starting a recipe, just in case there's an item you're allergic to. Daniel can eat these because they're peach-free!

1 Preheat the oven to 350°F (180°C) and line a muffin tray with 12 cupcake liners.

2 Peel the bananas and put them in a bowl, then mash them with a fork until almost smooth—it doesn't matter if there are a few little lumps in there.

3 Mix the brown sugar and vanilla extract into the banana purée, then add the eggs and oil, incorporating it all with a whisk.

4 Add the flour, baking powder, and baking soda and quickly fold everything together using a spatula until just combined. Be careful not to overmix or your muffins might be tough.

5 Once everything is mixed, use two spoons to spoon the batter into the cupcake liners, dividing it evenly between them. If you like, you can sprinkle the top of each muffin with a little bit of turbinado sugar.

6 Bake for about 20 minutes until risen and golden. Leave them to cool on a wire rack or enjoy warm from the oven.

> Try one, Prince Wednesday!

DF **VG** As these yummy cakes use oil and not butter, they are dairy-free. If you would like them to be vegan, too, use an egg substitute product; we suggest ½ cup of applesauce.

Baker Aker's Trolley Cookies

Preparation time: 40 minutes • Cooking time: 30 minutes • Makes about 30 cookies

INGREDIENTS

For the cookies:

⅔ cup (1⅓ stick/150 g) butter, softened

1½ cups (5½ oz/150 g) granulated sugar

1 egg

1 teaspoon vanilla bean paste or vanilla extract

2¼ cups (10½ oz/300 g) all-purpose flour, plus extra for dusting

1 teaspoon baking powder

For decorating:

1½ cups (7 oz/200 g) confectioners' sugar

Red food coloring

Candy, such as jellybeans, chocolate chips, sprinkles, etc.

Tubes of writing icing (optional)

Every step of this recipe is great fun: from rolling the dough and cutting out the trolley shapes to tasting the cookies when the oven goes *ding!*

1 To make the cookies, put the butter and sugar in a stand mixer and beat until light and fluffy.

2 Add the egg and vanilla and continue to beat until well combined.

3 Firmly but quickly mix in the flour and baking powder and bring it together into a ball. Be careful not to overmix, as it may make the cookies tough. Flatten the dough into a large patty, wrap it in plastic wrap, and chill for at least 30 minutes.

4 While the dough chills, preheat the oven to 350°F (180°C) and line two baking sheets with parchment paper.

5 Dust the work surface with a little flour and roll out the dough to about ⅛ inch (2 to 3mm) thick. Use a trolley or train-shaped cookie cutter to stamp out cookies and place them on the baking sheets. You can gather up the offcuts and reroll the dough to stamp out more cookies.

Continued...

Here comes Trolley—ding ding!

DF You don't have to use butter—a non-dairy spread will make these dairy-free.

GF Make these gluten-free by using a gluten-free all-purpose flour blend— and check your baking powder and candy are gluten-free, too!

6 Bake the cookies (you will probably need to do this in batches) for 9 to 11 minutes, or until pale golden. Allow to cool on the baking sheet for a few minutes, then transfer them to a wire rack to cool completely before decorating.

7 Once the cookies have cooled, put the confectioners' sugar into a shallow mixing bowl and add enough water to make a thick icing. Add the food coloring and mix in to make the icing red.

8 One at a time, hold a cookie upside down and dip the top of it into the red icing. Let all the excess drip off before placing the cookie, icing side up, on a tray.

9 Decorate the cookies with candy and sprinkles, perhaps adding jellybeans for headlights and chocolate chips for wheels. Once the red icing is dry, you could even try drawing on the seats, windows, or other features with tubes of writing icing, if you wish!

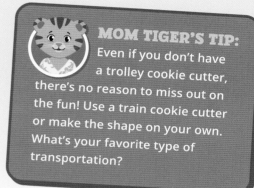

MOM TIGER'S TIP: Even if you don't have a trolley cookie cutter, there's no reason to miss out on the fun! Use a train cookie cutter or make the shape on your own. What's your favorite type of transportation?

Won't you ride along with us?

Daniel Tiger's Favorite Peanut Butter and Choc Chip Cookies

Preparation time: 15 minutes • Cooking time: 13 minutes • Makes 16 cookies

INGREDIENTS

- ¼ cup (½ stick/60 g) butter
- ¼ cup (2 oz/60 g) crunchy peanut butter
- ½ cup (3½ oz/100 g) granulated sugar
- ½ cup (3½ oz/100 g) light brown sugar
- 1 egg, beaten
- 1½ cups (7 oz/200 g) self-rising flour
- 1 cup (5¼ oz/150 g) milk chocolate chunks

These cookies definitely have the wow factor: yummy peanut butter one bite, then delish choc chips the next. Best washed down with cold milk.

1. Preheat the oven to 350°F (180°C) and line two baking sheets with parchment paper.

2. Beat together the butter, peanut butter, and both sugars in a large mixing bowl until light and fluffy (use a stand mixer or electric hand mixer, if you have one), then beat in the egg until well incorporated.

3. Now fold in the flour and chocolate chips until everything is combined—don't use an electric mixer for this. Just use a wooden spoon and your hands to bring it together. Tip the dough out onto a work surface and knead lightly to bring it together.

4. Divide the dough into 16 even portions and roll them into balls in the palms of your hands. Place the balls on the baking sheets (six on each), leaving a little space between them to spread out as they cook. Press the balls down a little so that they are flattened like patties.

5. Bake for about 12 to 13 minutes until lightly golden. Leave to cool on the baking sheets before enjoying.

Do you like cookies?

DF To make these dairy-free, use a non-dairy spread and dairy-free chocolate chips.

GF If you need to make them gluten-free, just substitute the regular self-rising flour for a gluten-free self-rising blend.

DAD TIGER'S TIP: If you have a peanut allergy, these cookies taste delicious with sunflower butter at a 1:1 ratio.

MOM TIGER'S TIP: If you just want to make a few and save a few for later, you can freeze the dough to cook another time. Freeze it in individual portions and just take out as many as you need from the freezer. Add a few minutes to the cooking time if cooking from frozen.

Nana Platypus's Mozies

Preparation time: 10 minutes • Cooking time: 20 minutes • Makes 12 cookies

INGREDIENTS

2 bananas, peeled

1½ cups (5½ oz/150 g) old-fashioned rolled oats

Scant 1 cup (2½ oz/70 g) dried shredded coconut

¼ cup (4 tablespoons) honey

⅓ cup (1¾ oz/50 g) raisins

When it comes to Nana Platypus's munchy mozies, one is never enough. Try dancing the raisins into the mixture, just like Daniel and Jodi did!

1 Preheat the oven to 350°F (180°C) and line a baking sheet with parchment paper.

2 Put the bananas in a mixing bowl and mush them to a purée with a fork.

3 Add the oats, coconut, and honey and mix everything together.

4 Add the raisins to the mixture—you can dance them into the mixture, like Daniel and Jodi do, if you like! Make sure that they are mixed in well.

5 Using a teaspoon, scoop spoonfuls of the mixture and blob them onto the baking sheet, spacing them a little apart. You should be able to make about 12. Flatten them down and neaten them a little so they form patties.

6 Place the mozies in the oven and bake for about 20 minutes until they are crisp and golden all over but still soft and gooey in the center.

Let's make a mozie treat together!

VG If you need to make these vegan, use maple syrup instead of the honey.

GF These are naturally gluten-free, but you may want to buy special gluten-free oats, to be on the safe side.

DAD TIGER'S TIP: Nana had run out of chocolate chips, but if you like, you can use chocolate chips instead of raisins for an extra special treat.

Chrissie's Chocolate Treat Puddles

Preperation time: 20 minutes • Cooking time: 5 minutes • Makes about 12 puddles

INGREDIENTS

3½ ounces (100 g) chocolate

Selection of chopped nuts, dried fruit, sprinkles, mini marshmallows, seeds, etc., for decorating

Once the hot water bit is out of the way, this is a recipe where the kids can really take charge. A bit messy, but lots of fun—with delish results!

1 Place the chocolate in a double boiler, or in a glass bowl set over a pan of simmering water, and melt slowly. Remove from the heat and let it cool for a few minutes so it thickens up a little bit.

2 Use a spoon to drizzle puddles of the chocolate onto a sheet of parchment paper.

3 While the chocolate is still wet, add your decorations of choice. Leave the chocolate to set in a cool place or the fridge before removing the puddles from the parchment.

I'm Chrissie, nice to know you!

MOM TIGER'S TIP: When buying chocolate for this, something a little on the dark side is best as it will set more firmly than milk chocolate.

DF **VG** Use a vegan, dairy-free chocolate for these, if you need to. And make sure any marshmallows or chocolate sprinkles are suitable, too!

Daniel Tiger's Birthday Cake

Preparation time: 2 hours • Cooking time: 25 minutes • Makes 1 large cake

INGREDIENTS

For the cake:

1⅓ cups (10½ oz/300 g) butter, softened, plus extra for greasing

1½ cups (10½ oz/300 g) granulated sugar

6 eggs

2¼ cups (10½ oz/300 g) all-purpose flour

3 teaspoons baking powder

Scant ⅔ cup (5 fl. oz./150 ml) milk

4 teaspoons vanilla extract

For the decoration:

1 heaping cup (2 sticks/250 g) butter

3¼ cups (1 pound/450 g) confectioners' sugar

2 tablespoons milk

1 tablespoon vanilla extract

1 tablespoon cocoa powder

Orange food coloring

Black, white, and red tubes of writing icing

The perfect cake for the Daniel Tiger fan in your family or neighborhood. Just don't expect any leftovers—it tastes even better than it looks!

1 Preheat the oven to 350°F (180°C) and grease and line two 9-inch (23-cm) square cake tins.

2 Put the butter and sugar into the bowl of a stand mixer (or into a large mixing bowl if you are using an electric hand mixer) and beat on high speed until light and fluffy.

3 Add the eggs two at a time, beating between each addition.

4 Sift the flour and baking powder together, then fold it into the batter mixture in two batches, alternating with half the milk each time. Fold the batter until everything is well incorporated.

5 Pour the mixture into the prepared tins and bake for 25 minutes, or until the cakes are risen and golden on top and a skewer inserted into the center of the cakes comes out clean. Leave to cool for a few minutes in the tins before turning out onto cooling racks to cool completely.

6 Meanwhile, make the buttercream. Put the butter into the stand mixer bowl (or large mixing bowl) and beat on high speed until it is whipped up. Add the confectioners' sugar, a little at a time, with the mixer on a slow speed.

7 Once the sugar is all incorporated, add the milk and vanilla. Turn the mixer up to high and whisk for another minute or so until the buttercream frosting is really light and fluffy.

Continued...

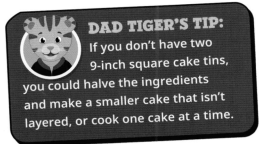

DAD TIGER'S TIP: If you don't have two 9-inch square cake tins, you could halve the ingredients and make a smaller cake that isn't layered, or cook one cake at a time.

DF If you need to make your cake dairy-free, use a plant-based spread instead of the butter and a plant-based milk, too.

8 Remove a couple of tablespoons of the frosting into a small bowl and add the cocoa powder to it. Mix together well—you will use this for Daniel's stripes. Cover the bowl and set aside.

9 Transfer another spoonful of the frosting to a separate small bowl and add enough food coloring to get a dark orange. With the mixer running, add the orange frosting back into the main bowl, a little at a time, stopping when the buttercream reaches the right shade of orange.

10 Returning to the cakes, level them if necessary, then spread a thin layer of frosting all over the top of one. Invert the other cake and place it on top, so that the top of the main cake is one of the flat bases.

11 Place an 8-inch round cake tin on top of the cake, positioning it to the bottom edge of the cake so that there's more space at the top. Gently draw around it with a knife to score the circle, but don't cut down too far.

12 Now, use a 3-inch cookie cutter to mark the ears at the top of the cake, positioning them, one on each side, half over the line of the main circular cake. Press down lightly, but don't go too deep. Once you have marked out your face with ears, cut around the whole outside with a small sharp knife.

13 Spread a very thin layer of the buttercream around the whole of the cake. This is called the crumb coat and will seal the cake and stop crumbs from getting into the final neat layer of frosting that will be on show. Pop the cake in the fridge to chill until the frosting is completely set.

14 Once the crumb coat is set, frost the cake again more neatly with the remaining icing and leave to set.

15 Now it's time to decorate! Using a palette knife (or even your finger if this is easier) daub stripes of the chocolate frosting on the cake to make Daniel's stripes. Look at his picture to see where the stripes should go. Use the chocolate frosting to also add the dark patches inside Daniel's ears.

16 Using the writing icing tubes, draw Daniel's face. Start with the black and draw the shape of his eyes and mouth, then use the red to draw his nose. Fill in his eyes with the white icing and draw on his whiskers!

MOM TIGER'S TIP: To make sure everything is in the right place, you can gently draw Daniel's features on lightly with a skewer before going over the lines in writing icing.

When's your birthday?

Grr-ific Recipe Round-Up

Hi, neighbor! It's time to say goodbye, but before you go, have fun answering these questions with your grown-up...

Which recipe in this book was the **YUMMIEST**?

Tell us why... _____

_____

_____

Which recipe in this book was the **MOST FUN** to make?

Tell us why... _____

_____

_____

Which recipe in this book was the **MESSIEST** to make?

Tell us why... _____

_____

_____

Which recipe in this book was your **FAVORITE**?

Tell us why... _____

_____

_____

Grown-Up Notes

Ugga mugga, neighbor!

123

Index

DINNERTIME LOOK & FIND ANSWERS
There are 7 carrots in the Tiger Family kitchen.
Did you spot them all and the other items, too?

Andrews McMeel Publishing
a division of Andrews McMeel Universal
1130 Walnut Street, Kansas City, Missouri 64106

www.andrewsmcmeel.com

22 23 24 25 26 SDB 10 9 8 7 6 5 4 3 2 1

ISBN: 978-1-5248-7611-1

Project Management and Design: Amazing15
Writer and Food Styling: Rebecca Woods
Additional Writing and Copy Editing: Kate Lloyd
Photography: Dan Scudamore

Editor: Erinn Pascal
Art Director: Holly Swayne
Production Editor: Margaret Utz
Production Manager: Tamara Haus
Coordinator – Consumer Products, 9Story: Ben Claar

Special thanks to Alysia Scudamore, Mikey Scudamore, and Hannah Scudamore.

Made by: King Yip (Dongguan) Printing & Packaging Factory Ltd.
Address and location of manufacturer:
Daning Administrative District, Humen Town
Dongguan Guangdong, China 523930
1st Printing—7/25/22